God's Plan to Financial Fitness

Foundational Principles of Financial Stewardship

RONTRELL DESHEA LYNCH

Copyright © 2018 Rontrell Deshea Lynch

All rights reserved.

ISBN: 1978318413
ISBN-13: 978-1978318410

DEDICATION

This book is dedicated to my beautiful wife and business partner Anita. I love that I get to do life with you.

CONTENTS

   Acknowledgments   i

   Introduction   1

1 Developing Resolve   3

2 Action   5

3 Changing Your Value System   8

4 An Action Plan for Debt   13

5 Assessment   17

6 Spending Plan   19

7 Where Do I Go From Here   23

ACKNOWLEDGMENTS

No one can accomplish or fulfill their assignment on their own, to think so would be asinine. Our lives are a result of the many relationships we have had over time and the deposits those individuals made.

To Dr. Bernard Grant, for being a godly example and seeing the greatness in me when I did not see it in myself. Thank you for challenging and stretching me.

INTRODUCTION

In order to become physically fit you must make certain lifestyle adjustments. This book is about adjustments and lifestyle changes. Diets rarely work because some find it very constraining. The same is true with financial fitness.

This book does not try to force some limiting lifestyle upon you whereby you hoard every dime that you have. What it does is target the areas in your life that require change. The word change means to renovate, transform, modify, adjust, amend and alter. Understand that change is a good thing and that God requires us to change for the better. Also keep in mind that forced changed is not lasting change. In other words, until change becomes important to you, you will eventually revert back to your current state.

In order to change you must be motivated to change. Motivation comes from goal setting. In this book I focus on goal setting and strategies that will allow you to reach those goals. One key point that I stress in this book is sacrifice. Take for example athletes that train. They deny themselves many things and train intensely. That intense training helps them reach their goals.

Goals must also be specific and not vague. Vague goals do not give you a clear target. Not only must you have goals, but you must develop plans and strategies to reach those goals. What is it going to take to reach them? What steps are you going to take? What is it that you may have to give up? Even though you are not required to live like a pauper to gain financial fitness, you have to give up some things.

What this book does is offer insight on how you can set these goals and tailor the steps to reach them to your unique situation. Be forewarned: change is not easy but you can do it if you decide, and the key to change is deciding. We make decisions every day. A decision is a choice or a resolution. Every choice we make has a result. These results can be either positive or negative. In order to live the life that God intended us to, we must have resolve and a bent towards the things of God. So it is with His plan to financial fitness. It begins with resolve.

Chapter 1

DEVELOPING RESOLVE

Have you ever wondered why some people are successful and others fail? The truth is that even successful people have actually failed. The only difference is that the successful person chooses not to give up. Successful people know that failure is not final. Many successful individuals have faced many disappointments before actually reaching their desired outcome in life.

Before I continue, I want to define what resolve is because the power to define is the power to fulfill. Resolve means to make a firm decision about; a fixed decision; to make up the mind; to find the answer or solution to.

Here are a few synonyms for the word resolve: determination, steadfastness, tenacity, firmness and doggedness. Now that I have defined resolve, lets determine how we develop it. If any of you have children or have a niece or nephew or grandchild you have probably experienced or witnessed great resolve. Resolve can often be observed in children. One of the first words we learn to say is no. Although misplaced sometimes, children can be very firm once they have determined to do or not to do something. We are all born with this resolve or this will to do or not to do.

Let us focus on the word will. The synonym for the word will that sticks out the most to me is self-control. A circular definition, yet very befitting for this subject is controlling self. I have learned in life that the only person you have and should have control over is you. With that being said, in order to develop resolve, one must first make a firm decision. Resolve begins with deciding. In deciding, one develops a will to stick with the decision. Lastly, one must develop self-control to be consistent in the determined course. How does this tie in with your finances? If you want to live a better life and live a more fulfilling life you must make a decision to do so. Say it with me, today I make a decision to make the necessary adjustments in order to live a more fulfilling life.

When faced with a financial situation at one point in my life, I asked God for His direction. His response was simply, "change your lifestyle." The answer to our financial problems is available, but it is up to us to make the decision to change as well as take action. Let us get back to self-control.

One way to gain the resolve you need to change your situation is to first envision yourself living the kind of life you want to live. Once you envision this life, think about the things you are doing currently. Do they fit into the type of life you want? Do they contribute to what you envision for your life or take you further away? Decide today that from this day forward you will not engage in any behavior that will abort your desired goal.

Let us embellish this thought of deciding, because deciding is not doing, deciding is determining. When you decide you need to change you become cognizant of the need for change, but you do not necessarily change. Consider the illustration of the five frogs sitting on the lily pad. John Maxwell uses this illustration in his book *The 15 Invaluable Laws of Growth*.

He states that four decided to jump off. How many are left? Some of you may say one. Although it may seem as if four jumped off, deciding is not necessarily doing. Albert Einstein stated that the definition of insanity is doing the same thing over and over again and expecting different results. I have come to the conclusion that insanity is also expecting results without doing anything at all. Once you have made a decision to change and have developed the resolve, then do it.

Chapter 2

ACTION

Most people converse quite often about starting a new diet or spending more time with their kids or taking up a new craft, but few do it. The next step in getting your finances together is to just simply do it. Do not continue to say that you would like to be able to save or get out of debt, just do it. One of the greatest gifts that God has given us is the human will. We can choose to not do anything or we can choose to do something. Either one of those choices will bring some type of outcome.

Our actions determine our success in life. I want to encourage you that those that have achieved financial freedom are no different from you. They just did the things that most people chose not to do. The definition of action is organized activity to accomplish an objective. So in order to accomplish the task of financial freedom you must focus your efforts in an organized manner. Many people think that activity equals productivity. You must have an action plan to get your finances together and your efforts must be focused. One action plan is a spending plan. I will talk about this more in depth in a later chapter. A spending plan is exactly what it states, a plan for your spending. If you do not tell your money where to go it will just go. Have you ever gotten your paycheck and the following week wonder what you did with it? Remember I told you that your decision to not do anything or to do something will have an outcome. Well, when you do not decide or plan how you will spend your money, it brings you a negative outcome. Also keep in mind that action is not necessarily productivity. You are spending your money paying your bills etc., but not in a focused manner. I try to live by the five Ps of planning. Proper Planning Prevents Poor Performance. The word performance means to act. The word act is the root word of action. So the opposite is true. Improper planning causes poor performance or action.

The law of diminishing intent states that the longer you wait to do a thing that you know you should do the more likely you will not do it. So the longer you wait to get your finances together the harder it becomes. Humans are habitual creatures: we tend to do things by habit. A habit is an action or pattern of behavior that is repeated so often that it becomes typical of somebody, although he or she may be unaware of it. A habit is not a bad thing, as a matter of fact if you want to change your financial situation you must develop new habits to correct your old ones. Most of us have developed bad spending habits, but these habits can be changed, subsequently new habits have to be developed.

I will talk further about the new habits that you need to develop in the chapters to come. I want to first of all get you to change the way that you think about money. Money is defined as a medium of exchange. Before currency was introduced we thrived on a barter system. I would have given you an item in exchange for another item of value. We no longer operate on this system so money is seen as something of value we exchange for something else of value. The term value is what I am trying to drive home. Something of value is defined as something of importance or significance. The first mental step in changing our habits is to change our value system. Matthew 6:21 teaches that where a man's heart is, his resources will follow or what you treasure the most or value is where you will spend your resources. Our actions are a product of our desires. Once you line your desires with actions that bring positive results and consistently do it, it then becomes a habit. God stated in Habakkuk 2:2 to write down the vison and make it plain or be specific. I will talk more about vision later, but visualization is a way to mentally go or be where you want without going there.

It does not cost you anything to dream. Visualization is synonymous with dreaming and it arouses desires. Therefore we must develop new values through visualization.

Chapter 3

CHANGING YOUR VALUE SYSTEM

Desire is a product of your association, so when trying to change your value system you must also be careful of the environment that you are in. If you were trying to lose weight, would you think it wise to constantly find yourself in a donut shop? No. Why not? Because being in that type of environment evokes in you a desire for that type of food. I am not saying that you hide from everything, but what I am saying is that until you build or develop the discipline to resist those things it is best to stay away from them. It is the same in the area of finances. If you know that every time you walk in the mall you are going to see that dress or those shoes that you "cannot live without", then you need to stay out of the mall! How do we build the discipline to resist the things that we love? It comes down to changing our value system.

What must happen is we must exchange our love for the things that bring us negative results, for the things that bring us positive results. Your desire to get out of debt or save or any other financial goal that you have set must replace those other desires. I am not saying that shopping is a bad thing, but you can do the right thing at the wrong time. I mentioned earlier in this book that I would touch on the subject of sacrifice. There may be a time when you have to sacrifice or go without certain things in order to meet or accomplish your dreams.

I talked about vision in the last chapter. It is important that you understand what vision is, because it is through vision or visualization that we change our value system. As discussed earlier, vision is a mental sight, a dream. One aspect of vision I want to focus on is a mental sight. Advertisers understand this concept of visualization. This is one reason why they invest millions of dollars into marketing their products. What you must begin practicing daily is visualization. See yourself out of debt, financially stable, all your needs met. So it begins with changing the way you see money and the purpose of money.

Changing the way you see money
As discussed earlier, money is a medium of exchange. But what is the purpose of money? I have an acronym for money to remind me of the purpose of money, G.I.S.S. The purpose of money is for giving, investing, saving and spending.

Giving

Someone may be saying, I thought that this book was about getting my finances together not giving them away. I understand where you are coming from, but keep in mind the title of this book, **God's Plan** to *Financial Fitness*. Understand that giving is a way to protect you against greed. Now greed is not wanting more, we should all want to do better and have more, but greed is wanting to have more for self alone. Giving opens you up to receive more. In his book *Halftime*, Bob Buford talks about a very successful executive who was seeking advice on how to live his life. The executive sought out a very well know Zen master. He began to tell the Zen master about his life and his business. The Zen master began to pour tea while the executive quieted himself. The Zen master poured the tea until it overflowed and spilled on the grass and across the mat towards the executive. The executive asked the Zen master what he was doing. The Zen master answered and stated "life is like this teacup flowing over, there's no room for anything new, you must pour out not take more in".

In order to gain the more in life we must remember to always empty ourselves. No, I am not saying give all that you have and live like a poor person. That would be the opposite of financial fitness. What I am saying is that you must leave room for giving in your budget. Giving is also God's way of blessing you. Giving is a law that God established to multiply and bring more into your life. Luke 6:38 states that if we give it will be given back to us. The thing I love about God is that when we give He multiplies what we give. For example, we can see God's law of giving in nature. When we take an apple seed and plant it in the ground we do not get just one apple in return, but we get an apple tree that has numerous apples. Always factor in the tithe (10 percent of your income and increase) and giving in your budget.

Investing

Investing is another component of money. Investing is the commitment of money in order to gain a financial return. What investing does is cause your money to grow. Investing is the opposite of working for money. Instead your money is working for you; whether it is investing in stocks, real estate or mutual funds. There are many books out there that can give you more insight into investing in these things. Always remember to not invest anything that you cannot afford to lose. Investing should come before spending but after you have your emergency fund. I will talk more about an emergency fund in the component of saving.

Saving

The next component of money is saving. You should save at least ten percent of your income and have at least a three to six-month emergency fund. Although circular, I define an emergency fund as a fund for emergencies. If you were to become unemployed or had some unforeseen emergency, this fund will allow you to live without having to borrow or use your credit cards. In Genesis 41:46-57, Joseph used this tactic to save numerous people during a famine.

This category can be seen on some spending plans as PYF or pay yourself first. I do not totally agree with this. I think that giving should be the first thing you put on your spending plan and you should center your budget around it. Giving is not the first component on my list by accident. I believe in PGF or pay God first and then yourself. As I explained, giving guards against greed and it is oftentimes easy to spend all of your money and not have anything left over for giving. Also before you invest, you must first make sure that you have your emergency fund intact. The order of investing second is assuming that your emergency fund has already been established.

Another reason you want to save is for major purchases. Credit card debt can be easy to get into but hard to get out of. Debt is the opposite of having your money work for you, instead your money is working in reverse. Credit card companies charge an average of 24 percent interest on your purchases if you do not pay the balance before the grace period. Just imagine how hard your money would have to work to pay off 24 percent interest. Which brings me to another point and I may as well talk about this while we are on the subject of debt. In comparing your financial fitness to natural fitness, there are a lot of things like special belts or clothing to make you appear slim, but once you take off these restricting garments you are still the same size. It is the same way with debt. It may make you look like you are doing alright but you really are not.

Spending

Now spending money as it relates to being a smart spender is what I want to focus on. I am pretty sure none of us have a problem with spending money, we all know how to do that. My focus on spending will be becoming a smart spender. Spending means to use up or put out, to pay out or disburse money. Department stores are geared towards women and let's face it, ladies, you love to shop! There is nothing wrong with spending if you are a planned spender versus an impulsive or emotional spender, as a matter of fact God tells us in I Timothy 6:17 that he richly provides us with things for our enjoyment. The goal of financial fitness, as I stated in the introduction, is not that you live like a poor person, but just the opposite; so you will have money to enjoy.

Emotional spenders on the other hand spend to make themselves feel better; much like comfort foods for those that eat to feel better. Impulsive spenders may or may not shop for emotional comfort, but their spending is not planned. In order to stick to your budget and have your money working for you, you must include spending in your budget. Normally when we do not include spending in our budget we normally use our credit cards to purchase the things that we want or even need. A budget helps guard against debt when we plan our spending and include it in our budget.

Chapter 4

AN ACTION PLAN FOR DEBT

Before we talk about an action plan for debt, let's look at what debt is and how it can potentially affect our plan to become financially fit. Let's define debt; debt is something that is owed or that one is bound to pay to or perform for another, a liability or obligation to pay or render something. What we do when we get into debt is obligate our monies. This is very similar to what economists call an opportunity cost. An opportunity cost is a benefit that could have been gained from an alternative use of the same resource. When we get into debt we forgo what we could have used our money for.

Remember the acronym G.I.S.S. I gave you in chapter three; the four main purposes for money: giving, investing, saving and spending. What debt does is limit the amount of money allocated to these areas of your life. You may be wondering how you can get anything without borrowing money to purchase it, i.e. a car or home. Let's talk about debt and I will allow you to make the decision about it. Let's say that we can't survive without debt and that we have to borrow for things like transportation and shelter. Let's take the stance that we have to have debt much like we have to have food in order to survive. Yes, we have to have food to survive, but we do have to eat the right types of food to be healthy. We also must limit the amount of food we consume because overindulgence is the main cause of obesity, which in turn can lead to a plethora of diseases.

Good Debt vs. Bad Debt

Bad Debt

Before we talk about good debt let's talk about bad debt. When we first moved into our home we accumulated a lot of debt. The majority of us get into the bulk of our debt once we purchase our home. You want to make sure that your home is fully furnished and decorated so you get all your furniture on credit. You also get your electronics on credit and get a department store credit card as well. You also begin to receive offers for credit cards in the mail and begin to accept those offers. The problem with debt is that it is easy to get into but hard to get out of. Much like how it is easy to gain weight but hard to lose it. You look at yourself in the mirror one day and think to yourself, how did I gain all this weight? It is not until you look at and assess where you are that you begin to take steps to change. We will talk about assessment later.

Credit card companies make it so easy for you to fall into this trap. Convenience and not having to wait; you can have what you want right now at the swipe of your card. What these companies do not tell you is that you will pay for this convenience and instant gratification. Most credit card companies lure you in with a low introductory rate or twelve months same as cash. What we fail to realize is that credit card companies are for profit and that they are in the business of making money. I think sometimes we think that these companies have our best interest.

These companies have shareholders and only have the shareholders best interest in mind. These shareholders invest in these companies and they expect a return on their investment. I don't think that the shareholders would be happy if credit card companies were not making any money for them. For example, if you accumulated $5,000 in credit card debt and you make the minimum payment of $150.00 a month (assuming an interest rate of 15% and determining your minimum payment by 3 to 5 percent of your balance) it would take you about 4 years to pay it off and you would pay a total of $6,507.80.

If you took that same $150.00 a month and deposited it

into an investment account that was paying an interest rate of 3% compounded daily, at the end of the same 4 years you would have amassed $7,659.36. The principal amount you would have invested would be $7,000 and the interest you would have accrued is $459.36. Let's look at God's take on debt. I believe God does not necessarily frown on debt, but He does want us to be informed of what debt does to us. Proverbs 22:7 tells us that the borrower is slave to the lender. Let's define the word slave; one who is subservient to or controlled by another, one who is subject to or controlled by a specific influence. One who works extremely hard.

These definitions are very interesting wouldn't you say? I especially like the last part, "one who works extremely hard". You see, God never intended for you to "slave" or acquire resources trough toil. What debt does is cause you to be a slave to your creditors. You work 2 to 3 jobs to pay your bills and to stay afloat. As I stated earlier, this is the opposite of having your money work for you. Bad debt is counterproductive to God's plan of financial fitness.

Good Debt

There is disagreement among many financial experts about good debt vs bad debt or debt in general. I will present my stance on the subject and allow you to make the decision. If you are like the average person you may not have money to purchase a car or home outright with cash, so you go to the bank and borrow the money, right? The bank in turn gives you the money to purchase the home car etc. So now the bank has a lien on your car or a deed of trust on your home. In a nutshell, these instruments just give the bank the legal right to take back either the car or home if you default or do not pay them back. I want to present several stances on good debt; debt if used wisely can allow you to purchase the things that you need like a car or home and debt can be used as leverage to bring you passive income (income from rental activity or "trade or business activities in which you do not materially participate").

Let's talk about the first stance. We all need things like transportation and housing right? As I stated above, most of us are not in a position now (because the ultimate goal is to position yourself to pay cash for everything and be debt free) that we can pay cash for a home or car. When buying these things you cross from good to bad debt when you do not borrow wisely. Wise borrowers only get what they can afford at the time. As I stated in the section on bad debt, debt is not to be used to purchase things that you cannot afford in order to look rich. The line between good debt and bad debt gets crossed when you try to live above your means. We will talk more about living within your means later.

Chapter 5

ASSESSMENT

Assessment is a very important component to achieving financial fitness. When you assess where you are it forces you to do just that, see where you are. In order to change, we must see that there is a need for change. Many times we don't do things because we are not aware that we need to change. We continue to do the same thing without taking the time to think. Assessment forces you to analyze and think. Thinking or contemplation causes you to question your current state. Assessment also helps you to see where you currently are in order to set goals for change.

Normally when you desire to lose weight you either take a look at your current weight and you take a before picture. This will help you measure your progress and set a target or goal. When you are assessing your financial state, first begin by gathering all of your monthly expenses. Your expenses are broken down into two categories; fixed and variable. Fixed expenses are expenses that cost the same each month like your rent, mortgage or car payment. Variable expenses are expenses that change from month to month like groceries and utilities. In relation to assessment, viewing your current expenses helps you see how much you are spending and maybe some areas where you can cut down on spending.

Now that you have assessed your expenses, let's take a look at your current income. Much like your expenses, your income may be broken into the categories fixed and variable. Fixed income is income from stable constant monthly resources like your salary or wages. Variable income is income that is not stable; mostly self-employment income from a business in which you offer goods or services. In chapter four I talked about an action plan for debt. Remember I said that assessment helps you visualize where you are in order to set goals. Well one way you can see these goals come to fruition is through a spending plan.

Chapter 6

SPENDING PLAN

A spending plan will help you reach the goals that you set. It forces you to visualize on paper and properly plan your spending. A spending plan is needful for debt reduction and helping you live within your means. Now that you have gathered the items discussed in chapter five (expenses and income), let's take those items and create a spending plan. See the sample spending plan below:

Sample Spending Plan

Income:

	Planned	Actual
Work	2,000	1,500
Total Income	2,000	1,500

Fixed Expenses:

Rent	750	750
Car Payment	350	350
Total Fixed Expenses	1,100	1,100

Variable Expenses:

Utilities	250	300
Groceries	150	200
Total Variable Expenses	400	500

Amount Left:	500	-100

Notice in the top column we have planned and actual because this is a spending plan and plans sometimes don't work out the way we plan. So if you don't hit your target don't get discouraged just continue to work at it. So let's begin with our planned items. In the prior chapter I told you to gather your income both fixed and variable. So in the income column put in your expected wages both fixed and variable. Keep in mind that if you have variable income it will not normally be the same, so you must estimate this amount. Now add your income to find your total income.

Now go down to the expense column and put in your expenses. Remember in the prior chapter I told you that your expenses are broken in two categories fixed and variable. Put your fixed expenses like rent, mortgage, car payment in the fixed expense column and items like utilities and groceries in the variable expenses column. Remember that your variable expenses will have to be estimated so always over estimate them.

Next add up all of your expenses and subtract them from your total income to see what amount you have left. Let's stop here for a second, the amount you have left will determine your target goals. Normally a spending plan is done until all the projected income is spent, but I want to address a couple of things before we move on. As I stated, when developing a spending plan, you normally spend down all your money and allocate until there is 0 left in the amount left over. I want you to take a moment to see what your amount left over is, because that is what's going to determine your plan of action. You may be saying that you don't have anything left over, well we must see which areas we can scale down.

I believe that your spending plan should be planned around giving and saving. As I discussed in chapter three, you must change your value system; well giving and saving should be at the top of your list in relation to becoming financially fit God's way. So now plug into your budget 10 percent of your income for giving and 10 percent for saving as well as a discretionary offering. Now structure your spending plan around these two things. Your amount left over has probably changed tremendously. The purpose of this exercise is to get you to locate yourself and see where your money is going and to gain control of your finances.

Now that you have completed your spending plan and placed in all your debt, income, giving and saving, let's take a look at an action plan to rectify any negative outcomes. In order to rectify or correct a negative amount left over you must either take a look at ways you can skim down like maybe downsizing your cable plan or other variable expenses.

Another way to rectify this is to look at ways to earn extra income, which should only be a temporary fix to get you out of the situation that you are in. I believe that you shouldn't have to sacrifice time with family and friends for financial gain; and besides, it doesn't matter how much money you make it's what you do with it that counts.

Needs vs Wants

Now that we have developed a spending plan let's determine what areas you need to adjust to pay off bad debt. Before we look at the areas that you must adjust, lets define or compare the terms need and want. A need is defined as something that must be supplied for a certain condition to be maintained or a desired state to be achieved, a necessity or an obligation. A want is more relative. A want is a strong feeling to have something. You and I may need food, shelter and clothing to live, but do we need expensive clothing or do we need to eat out every day? When trying to work on your spending plan you must develop a need versus want mindset.

Do you need to have a thing or do you want it? A need versus a want attitude is about discipline. Remember this book approaches finances like that of physical fitness. Sometimes to be physically fit you must watch what you eat and make sure you exercise. You may want to eat certain foods, but they may not be healthy for you or they may keep you from reaching the goals you have as it relates to your health.

Chapter 7

WHERE DO I GO FROM HERE

I have learned in life that what we plan does not always happen the way we, well, plan it to happen. The key to achieving your goals is to continue to stick with them even when you fail. It is like when you are trying to lose weight or exercise. You may stick to a specific regimen for several days, but once the excitement wears off and you don't see results you quit. One thing I want you to know is that you are no different than anyone else.

If others have achieved financial fitness then you can as well. We sometimes feel like athletes and other successful people have some type of magic formula or we can never do what they do. I have learned that the only difference is that they continued to work hard at their craft even when it got hard and yes, they failed. The way you accomplish your goals is to realize that you may fail, but failure is not final. I like to live by the ideal that you only fail when you quit.

If you are still living and breathing there is always opportunity to accomplish your dreams and becoming financially fit should be one of those dreams. Imagine how much of a blessing you could be if your finances were in order. You would have more freedom to do the things that you love as well as be a blessing to others. Continue to apply the things in this book and don't get discouraged if you get off track. Just remember that anything worthwhile takes sacrifice and getting your finances in order is a very worthwhile thing and it can bring you great satisfaction. Congratulations on taking the first steps on your path to God's plan to financial fitness!

ABOUT THE AUTHOR

    Rontrell Deshea Lynch is a speaker and entrepreneur and has a passion for business and finances. Before becoming an entrepreneur and starting several businesses, he spent 10 years in the banking industry as a Senior Lending Officer.

    He has a Bachelor's in Business Administration and a Master of Finance with a concentration of Financial Planning. Rontrell uses the experience and knowledge he has gained to help others achieve their financial goals.

www.ingramcontent.com/pod-product-compliance
Lightning Source LLC
Chambersburg PA
CBHW050035230526
45470CB00003B/1292